Sip, Serve, Succeed: It's Your Time!
-Written By-
Jessica Jones

Copyright © 2024 Jessica Jones
Facebook: Author Jessica Jones

Cover Design: Danielle Tillman
Editor: Tamyra L. Griffin

All rights reserved. No part of this book may be used or reproduced in any form or by any means electronic or mechanical, including photocopying, recording or by information storage and retrieval system, without the written permission from the publisher and writer.

Because of the dynamic nature of the Internet, and Web addresses or links contained in this book may have changed since publication and may no longer be valid. The views expressed in this work are solely those of the author and do not necessarily reflect the views of the publisher and the publisher hereby disclaims any responsibility for them.

Acknowledgements

I first would like to Acknowledge My Lord & Savior for giving me the desires of my heart, and the courage to become an author, and whatever else I want to be.

"I can do all things through Christ which Strengthens Me" - Philippians 4:13

Next, I would like to thank my mother Sonya Elizabeth, who is also my fashion designer for always believing in me and having my back. I would like to recognize My daughter Lamiah for changing my life for the better. My entire family for being y'all. You don't get to choose your family, but God picked the perfect ones for me.
Thank You to my Graphic and most Elegant all the way around designer Danielle Tillman. I wouldn't be here without you. Thank You to my editor Tamyra Griffin for helping put this book together, for your patience, and paying it forward. Special shout out to Cordoba Photography. You helped me with my confidence in these shots.

Finally, I would like to Thank My Team at Bar247. We have been in good business going on 7 years, and each of you has brought me much joy working with you.

I love you all.
Jessica Jones

ITS YOUR TIME!

Hey there, future bartenders and business owners! I'm Jessica Jones, and I'm thrilled to take you on an exciting journey through the world of bartending and entrepreneurship. From my early days helping at my parent's lively parties to landing my first bartending gig at LAX airport, I've always had a passion for serving others and creating unforgettable experiences.

Fast Forward to 2018, and I've turned that passion into reality with Bar247, my very own Mobile bartending business serving all Southern California- and we're expanding! In this book, I'm sharing everything I've learned along the way, from the art of crafting classic cocktails to the ins and outs of running a successful mobile bar.

Get Ready to dive into the fascinating world of alcohols, learn the secrets of mixology, explore the wonders of beer and wine and uncover the essential skills needed to launch and grow your very own bartending business. My goal is to inspire and empower you to follow your dreams and succeed in this dynamic industry.

So, grab a shaker, raise your spirits, and let's embark on this incredible adventure together! I can't wait to help you discover the joy of bartending and excitement of entrepreneurship. Cheers to your future success!

Bar247

SETTING THE Bar

On this page I'm going to give you the basic bar utensils you need to bartend using your own set up. You can find these items on Amazon.

 **Muddler**

Shaker
A container used for mixing, chilling, and straining cocktails

Muddler
Used to crush and mix ingredients like herbs, fruits, and sugar in the bottom of the glass or shaker to release flavors and essential oils

Jigger
A double sided measuring tool used in bartending to accurately portion and pour liquid ingredients for cocktails

Bar Spoon
Are essential for gently combining ingredients and creating layered drinks with precision and control

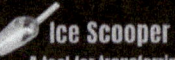 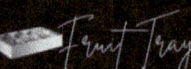 

Ice Scooper
A tool for transferring ice

Fruit Tray
Used to display a selection of fresh fruits and garnishes used in cocktails

Pourers
A double sided measuring tool used in bartending to accurately portion and pour liquid ingredients for cocktails

Bar Caddy
A organizer used to store and display essential bar tools, such as straws, napkins, stirrers, and other accessories for bartending

Juice Containers
Used to store and dispense various types of fruit juices, mixers or syrups commonly used in cocktail preparation

Mobile Bar Station
A portable setup equipped with essential bar tools, equipment, and supplies for preparing and serving cocktails at events

Glass Rimmer
Used to coat the rim of cocktail glasses with salt, sugar, or other flavorful garnishes

 Business Cards
Always have them on you!

 Liquor Liability Insurance
Necessary when running your business

TIPS + TRICKS

1. QR codes for tip and payments
Your cashapp tag and zelle tag which can both be found in your mobile banking apps

2. Always consult with the customer
Common questions include: Who is responsible for providing the alcohol? Do you have preferred cocktails you would like served? How many guest are you having?

3. Customer Service
As a courtesy, I always provide water free of charge as I like my guests to stay hydrated. You want to do your best to know your customers had a good time and getting home safe.

4. Offer Packages
I have two packages: Customers can pay me to shop for them, or they can provide everything and pay for services rendered. Always give customers your go to options and make suggestions. Communication is key!

5. Bonus Tips
Always bring sanitizing wipes, a towel to wipe down the bar, tip jar, and trash bags. It's great to have fruit garnishes cut, and prepped before you get to your event, I always suggest the day before.

6.
Make sure you know the number of guests you will be serving. This will help you determine the appropriate quantity of alcohol, juices, and mixers needed. You'll develop your own rhythm and process over time, and as you gain experience, you'll discover additional elements to incorporate. CHEERS!

Bar Measurements & Bar Slang

Conversion Chart:

1 ounce= 2 tablespoons. When free pouring, it's a four count. 1 Mississippi 2 Mississippi 3 Mississippi 4 Mississippi.

Yes, that's the base of it. Most cocktails are made starting with an ounce. If someone orders a shot, it's one ounce. If they want a double, 2 ounces. Let's move on.

3/4 oz= 1.1/2 tablespoon
1/2 oz = 1 tablespoon
1/4 oz = 1/2 tablespoon
2 oz= 1/4 cup
3 oz= ¼ cup + 2 tablespoons
4 oz=1/2 cup
6 oz= ¾ cup
8 oz= 1 cup
16 oz= 2 cups
24 oz= 3 cups
32 oz= 1 quart

Abbreviations Key

Ounce(s) = oz.
Tablespoon(s)= Tbsp.
Teaspoon(s)=tsp.
Cup= C

Bar Slang:

Build - To make a drink in the glass you are serving in. The first step is usually to fill the glass with ice.
Back - Nonalcoholic drink served on the side, such as water or soda.
Call drink - A drink that could be made at any bar. (i.e. Long Island Iced Tea).
Cocktail – A drink that combines one or more alcohol beverages.
Cordial or Liqueur- Obtained from the infusion of fruits, herbs, spices and other plants with liquor such as whiskey or brandy.
Dash - Smallest bar measurement.
Dry - Refers to the quantity of vermouth in a cocktail. Using less dry vermouth will result in a drier cocktail.
Float - Carefully pouring a small amount of liquid over the back of a spoon to balance as the top layer of a drink.
Libation - Beverages containing alcohol.
Liquor- Beverage distilled from alcohol.
Mixed Drink – Drink that combines one or more alcoholic beverages.
Mixer - Any non-alcoholic beverage used as an ingredient in a cocktail.
Muddle - Combining ingredients in the bottom of a glass using a muddler.
Neat - A drink served without ice or a mixer.
On the Rocks - Drink served over ice
Straight up - Drink chilled in a cocktail shaker and strained.
Sweet & Sour Mix - Mixture of lemon, lime and sugar commonly used in mixing cocktails.
Fermentation - The key step in the production of beer, wine, and spirits. Yeast is the microorganism primarily responsible for alcoholic Fermentation. When yeast consumes the sugars in the

raw material (such as malted barley for beer, grapes for wine, or grains for spirits), it produces alcohol and carbon dioxide as byproducts.

These days people make up new bar slang as well as cocktails that's been around for ages they add their own name to them. As you grow in the industry you will learn different slang as well as your own count when it comes to measuring or free pouring.

Region, and Distillation Process

Hey bartenders, I just wanted to give you a little background on the process of making the liquor. Where most spirits are made, and the process of them. We will start with Whiskey - it's the most distinct, and literal.

'And I'm off the CC' – Drake. CC is Canadian Club which is a Canadian whiskey.

Canadian Whiskey:
Typically made from a blend of grains - including corn, Rye, and barley and distilled in Canada. Often lighter and smoother compared to other types of whiskey aged in oak barrels for a minimum of 3 years.

Scotch Whiskey:
Made from Malted Barley and distilled primarily in Scotland. Distilled twice in pot stills, although some are distilled 3 times. Aged in Oak barrels for a minimum of 3 years. Sub types include single malt, single Grain, Blended malt, Blended Grain, and blended Scotch Whiskeys.

Irish Whiskey:
Made from a mix of malted and un-malted barley; and distilled in Ireland. Typically, triple distilled for smoothness. Aged for at least 3 years, often in ex bourbon or sherry casks.

Rye Whiskey:
Made from a mash bill that is at least 51% rye and distilled in the US - particularly in the Northeastern states and Canada. Aged in New charred oak barrels. Known for its spicy and fruity flavor profile.

Bourbon:
Primarily made from corn at least 51% and distilled in the US with most production centered in Kentucky. Aged in New charred oak barrels. The charring of the oak barrels caramelizes the natural wood sugars, adding depth and complexity to the distilled spirit.

The bourbon matures in the oak barrels, gradually developing flavors from the wood, as well as undergoing oxidation and evaporation. The aging period can vary, but it must be at least two years to be labeled as straight bourbon. Once the bourbon has reached its desired flavor profile through aging, it is removed from the barrels, filtered, and then bottled for distribution and consumption.

Tennessee Whiskey:
Like the bourbon but undergoes an additional filtration process known as the Lincoln County process - where the whiskey is filtered through charcoal before aging.

Japanese Whiskey:
Modeled after Scotch Whiskey, with a focus on quality and craftsmanship. Made in Japan, and often incorporates traditional Scottish methods. Known for its complexity and balance.

Let's Move on to Tequila - one of my Favs in taste. "Patron on the Rocks, that's what I'm on." – Drake. Okay, I'm done. Lol

Tequila:
Is a distilled alcoholic beverage made from the blue agave plant, primarily produced in the area surrounding the city of Tequila in the Jalisco State of Mexico. There are several types

of tequila, each with its own unique characteristics based on the production process and aging.

1. ***Blanco (Silver or Plata) Tequila:***
Clear and unaged tequila, typically bottled shortly after distillation. Fresh and crisp, with the agave flavor being prominent.

2. ***Reposado Tequila:***
Reposado means rested in Spanish. Aged in oak barrels for a minimum of two months and up to a year.
Develops a smoother and more complex flavor profile with notes of oak from the barrel aging.

3. ***Anejo Tequila:***
Aged in Oak barrels for a minimum of one year and up to three years. Rich and complex, with pronounced oak, vanilla, and caramel flavors. The longer aging imparts a darker color and a smoother, more refined taste.

Also, **Extra Anejo Tequila** - which was established in 2006 the year my kid was born - has a darker color from its rich notes of wood, caramel, and dark chocolate.

Tequila is made through a specific production process, which includes harvesting the blue agave, cooking the agave hearts (pinas), extracting the juices, fermenting the liquid, distilling the alcohol, and aging the tequila in barrels. The traditional method of production involves the use of brick ovens for cooking the agave, stone mills for extracting the juice, and copper pot stills for distillation.

Okay, it's Vodka time. Although I don't drink this as often, this is the go-to for cocktail recipes. You can shake up so many drinks with vodka. Have fun with it.

Vodka:
Vodka is a popular distilled spirit known for its neutral flavor profile and versatility in cocktails. It can be made from a variety of ingredients such as grains, potatoes, or even fruits. While Vodka is associated with Russia and Poland, it is produced in many countries around the world. Let's get into some common types of vodka.

Grain Vodka:
Made from such as wheat, rye, or barley. Known for its smooth and clean taste, often with a subtle sweetness. Produced in various countries, including Russia, Poland, and the U.S.

Potato Vodka:
Made from potatoes - which can impart a creamy, earthy, and slightly sweet flavor to the spirit. Historically associated with eastern European countries like Poland and Ukraine.

Wheat Vodka:
Specifically made from wheat, which can result in a soft, slightly sweet and creamy flavor profile. Commonly produced in Scandinavian countries, including Sweden and Finland.

Rye Vodka:
Distilled from Rye grains, providing a slightly spicy and robust flavor profile. Originates from countries such as Russia and Poland.

Corn Vodka:
Made from Corn, which can contribute a slightly sweet and mellow flavor. Often produced in the U.S.

Flavored Vodka:
Vodka infused with natural or artificial flavors such as citrus, berry, vanilla, or pepper. Widely available and used in a variety of cocktails.

Vodka Production typically involves distilling the base ingredient to a high level of alcohol purity and then diluting it with water to achieve the desired proof. The exact production methods can vary between distilleries, and some producers may use multiple distillation states or filtration processes to further refine the spirit. Vodka can be distilled in many countries around the world, with notable regions including Russia, Poland, Sweden, Finland, The U.S. and various other countries where distilleries have embraced the production of this globally popular spirit.

Gin

Alright Gin lovers, this is another Spirit that should be mixed really well - especially when making a martini.

London Dry Gin:
A classic style of gin that does not have to be made in London Typically Characterized by a strong Juniper flavor and a dry profile. It can be produced in various locations, not just limited to London.

Plymouth Gin:
A specific style of Gin with a protected geographical indication - meaning it must be made in Plymouth, England. Known for its slightly earthy and less Juniper forward flavor compared to London dry Gin.

Old Tom Gin:

Historically Popular in 18th Century England, Old Tom Gin is slightly sweeter than London Dry Gin. It experienced a revival in the craft cocktail movement and is produced by various distilleries.

Genever (Jenever)

Originating from the Neverlands and Belgium, Genever is considered the predecessor of modern gin. It has a maltier and more pronounced grain flavor due to its base spirit, which is often distilled from malted grains.

New Western Style American Style Gin:

A Newer Style of Gin that places less emphasis on Juniper and allows for a broader range of botanical flavors to come through. Distilled in Various locations, including the U.S and other countries that have embraced the craft gin movement.

International Gins:

Gins are produced in many countries around the world, each with its own local botanicals and flavor profiles. For example, Spain has seen a rise in the production of unique gin flavored with local ingredients.

Gin is distilled in numerous locations globally, and its production has expanded significantly beyond its historical roots in England, and the Netherlands. Many craft distilleries around the world are experimenting with botanicals and production methods to create unique and innovative gins, contributing to the diversity of the Spirit.

Cognac:

Cognac is a very powerful spirit the late great Tupac Shakur referred to as a role model. Lol. "They want to know who's my Role Model, it's in the brown bottle - Hennessy." Let's Go!

V.S. (Very Special) Cognac:
- Aged for a minimum of two years in oak barrels. Often used for mixing in cocktails due to its vibrant and youthful character.

V.S.O.P (very superior old pale) Cognac:
- Aged for a minimum of four years, although many qualities, V.S.O.P cognacs are aged longer. They're known for their smoothness and complexity, making them suitable for sipping or mixing in cocktails.

X.O (Extra Old) Cognac:
- Aged for a minimum of 10 years - although many X.O cognacs are aged significantly longer. Renowned for their riches, depth, and complexity. Often enjoyed as a sipping spirit.

Extra Cognac:
Represents the highest level of aging, with no specific minimum age requirement. Known for its exceptional depth, complexity, and richness. Often considered a luxurious and indulgent spirit.

Cognac is exclusively distilled in the cognac region of France, which is divided into six sub-regions: Grande Champagne, Petite Champagne, Borderies, Fins Bois, Bon Bois, and Bois Ordinaires. The unique Combination of climate, soil and expertise in these regions contribute to the distinctive character of cognac.

The production of cognac follows a specific process, from the selection and harvesting of grapes to distillation in copper pots, stills, and aging in oak barrels. The resulting spirit is celebrated for its smoothness, complexity, and the rich array of flavors that develop during the aging process.

Rum:

Rum is produced in various regions around the world, including the Caribbean, Latin America, and other tropical regions where sugarcane is grown. The fermentation process for rum begins by extracting sugarcane juice or using molasses, a byproduct of sugar production. Yeast is then added to the juice or molasses to ferment the sugars and convert them into alcohol. After fermentation, the liquid is distilled to separate the alcohol from the water and other impurities. The distillation process can vary, but it typically involves using copper pots stills or column stills to create a clear, high-proof spirit. Overall, rum production involves a combination of regional influences, fermentation of sugarcane-derived products, and distillation processes that contribute to the unique flavors and characteristics of different types of rum.

Next, we'll dive a little into Mezcal - not too deep however. I would like for my future bartenders to know the difference between Mezcal and tequila. And I feel it's important to recognize the tasting notes: smoky, sweet, earthy, spicy, vegetal, floral, anise, vanilla, fruity.

Mezcal:

The difference between Tequila and Mezcal is that tequila can only be made from the blue agave plant while mezcal can be made from any agave plant. Mezcal means cooked & agave. The process of making mezcal typically begins with harvesting mature agave plants, which are then roasted in underground pits. Once the agave hearts, or pinas, are cooked, they are crushed, and the juice extracted.

During Fermentation the extracted juice is placed in large wooden vats or barrels and left to ferment. During fermentation, natural yeasts in the air interact with the sugars in the juice, producing alcohol. After fermentation, the liquid is distilled in copper stills to concentrate the alcohol content and create a clear, smooth spirit. The distillation process involves heating the liquid and collecting the alcohol vapor, which is then cooled back into a liquid form. Overall, the combination of distillation and fermentation is what gives mezcal its unique flavor profile and character. The careful balance of these processes is what separates mezcal from other spirits and makes it a beloved drink around the world.

Types of Mezcal varieties:

Joven

- Can be aged up to 2 months. Has a smoky taste.

Reposado

- Ages for a minimum of 2 months but no longer than a year in oak barrels.

Anejo

- Aged for a minimum of one year but up to 3 years, this mezcal has a dark amber color with rich complexities for taste.

This concludes our distillation and fermentation process. Moving on to mixing Cocktails - where I show y'all how to cook it up. Lol!

COCKTAIL TIME

Okay guys we are going to get into making some classic tasty cocktails.

These are some of my favorites minus the Gin. I'll tell you a little story about that. I was 16 years old for the first time drinking but for some reason, I wanted to show out and act like it wasn't. We were at my friend's house having a gathering. Some guys came over with a bottle of Seagram's gin, and orange juice. I'm sure you can guess what happened next. Smh!

This guy is daring me to go shot for shot with him, well I did and ended up sick for 3 days. I got into so much trouble my mom couldn't tell what was wrong with me. I was barely moving or talking. She dragged it out of my best friend. I think my mom thought I was pregnant or something Ha Ha not funny then. Hilarious now.

Liqueurs

Time to get into some Liqueurs. These are mainly for mixed drinks - like a margarita you would use Grand Marnier, Cointreau, Or Triple Sec. However, there are a lot of shooters that are just Liqueur based. We will get into shooters later though.

Liqueurs are made by combining a base spirit with various flavoring agents such as fruits, herbs, spices, and botanicals. The base spirit can be derived from a variety of sources, including grains, fruits, or sugarcane. The flavoring agents are steeped in the spirit and then sweetened with sugar or syrup. Common liqueurs Include:

Grand Marnier:
A type of liqueur known as a triple sec, made from a blend of Ugni Blac Grapes, which are double distilled in copper stills. The resulting spirit is then aged in French oak barrels. The bitter orange essence is obtained from the peels of Caribbean oranges, and it is combined with the Cognac and sugar to create the distinctive flavor of Grand Marnier. The liqueur has a rich, velvety texture and a balanced, complex flavor with notes of orange, vanilla, and caramel. It is often used in cocktails and culinary preparations, adding depth and sweetness to a variety of dishes.

Amaretto:
A sweet Italian liqueur with a distinct almond flavor. It is made from a base of apricot pits or almonds, which are infused in neutral spirits, along with a combination of herbs and spices. The infusion is then sweetened with sugar, resulting in a rich

and complex almond taste with hints of vanilla and caramel. Amaretto can be enjoyed on its own as a digestif or used as a key ingredient in cocktails such as the Amaretto Sour or the Godfather. It is also commonly used in baking and dessert recipes to add depth and sweetness to dishes.

Baileys Irish Cream:
A popular liqueur that originated in Ireland. It is made from a blend of Irish Whiskey, fresh dairy cream, cocoa, and vanilla flavors. The whiskey used in Baileys is sourced from various distilleries in Ireland and provides a smooth and distinctive base for the liqueur. The fresh dairy cream is carefully selected to ensure a rich and creamy texture, while the cocoa and vanilla flavors add depth and sweetness to the blend. Baileys Irish Cream is known for its indulgent taste and can be enjoyed on its own over ice, mixed into coffee or cocktails, or used in dessert recipes.

Kahlua:
A coffee-flavored liqueur that originated in Mexico. It is made from rum, sugar, vanilla, and arabica coffee beans. The process of making Kahlua involves steeping the coffee beans in the rum to extract their flavors along with the addition of sugar and vanilla for sweetness and depth. The resulting liqueur has a rich and complex coffee taste with notes of caramel and vanilla. Kahlua is versatile and can be enjoyed on its own over ice, mixed into cocktails like White Russians and Espresso Martinis, or used in dessert recipes to add a hint of coffee flavor.

Cointreau:
A premium French orange liqueur known for its clear color and intense orange flavor. It is made from a blend of sweet and bitter orange peels, which are distilled with alcohol to extract

the essential oils and aromas. These oils are then blended with sugar and pure alcohol to create the final liqueur. Cointreau has a bright and zesty flavor with hints of citrus and a smooth, balanced sweetness. It is commonly used in cocktails such as the Margarita, Cosmopolitan, and Sidecar - where its vibrant orange notes enhance the overall flavor profile. Cointreau is also a popular choice for desserts and culinary preparations, adding a sophisticated touch of citrus to dishes.

Frangelico:
A delicious Italian hazelnut liqueur with a rich and nutty flavor profile. It is made from Tonda Gentile hazelnuts, which are harvested in the Italian region of Piedmont. The hazelnuts are toasted to release their oils and flavors, then infused in alcohol along with cocoa, vanilla, and other botanicals. The infused mixture is sweetened with sugar and distilled to create the smooth and velvety liqueur known as Frangelico. This liqueur has a distinct hazelnut aroma and taste with undertones of cocoa and vanilla. Frangelico is often enjoyed on its own, over ice, or as a key ingredient in cocktails and dessert recipes, adding a deliciously nutty and sweet flavor.

SH⬤TS!

Shots Shots Shots Shots Shots Shots Shots shots Shots Shots!

Everybody!!! (singing)

*Alright Alright Alright! (Kevin Hart Daddy Voice)

Time to get into some shooter cocktails Just some of my favs I feel your customers will enjoy.

APPLE PIE

Ingredients:
- 1 shot Vodka
- 1 shot apple juice
- 1 dash of cinnamon

Instructions:
Fill shot glass with vodka and apple juice

Sprinkle cinnamon on tongue and pour contents of shot glass into mouth, swirl ingredients in mouth to mix in cinnamon.

BLOW JOB

Ingredients:
- ½ Baileys (Irish cream)
- ¼ oz Kahlua (Coffee Liqueur)
- Whipped cream

Instructions:
Pour liqueurs into a shot glass and top with whipped cream, have an individual put his/her hands behind his/her back, then have him/her pick up the shot glass with his/her mouth, tilt head back slowly, and Shoot.

B-52

Ingredients:
- 1/3 oz Baileys (Irish Cream)
- 1/3 oz Kahlua (coffee Liqueur)
- 1/3 oz amaretto (almond Liqueur)

Instructions:
Layer ingredients in order into the shot glass. And Shoot!

CARAMEL APPLE

Ingredients:
- ½ oz Sour Apple Pucker Schnapps
- ½ oz butterscotch schnapps

Instructions:
Add Ice to shaker pour in ingredients. Strain into a shot glass. And shoot!

DUCK FART

Ingredients:
- ½ oz Kahlua (coffee liqueur)
- ½ oz baileys (Irish cream)
- ½ oz Crown Royal (Canadian whiskey)

Instructions:
Layer ingredients in order into a shot glass.
And Shoot!

KOOL AID

Ingredients:
- 1 shot Vodka
- 1 shot sloe gin
- 1 shot triple sec
- 1 shot amaretto (almond liqueur)
- Cranberry juice

Instructions:
Pour ingredients in a large glass with ice and shake, pour into shot glass add cranberry juice. And Shoot!

Remember guys all these shooter cocktails are served chilled straight up no ice goes into the shot glass. Enjoy!!!

Whiskey Cocktails

Whiskey Smash

Ingredients:
2 oz Bourbon or whiskey
3/4 oz fresh lemon juice
¾ oz simple syrup
4-5 fresh mint leaves

Instructions:

1. In a shaker combine ingredients.
2. add 4-5 mint leaves.
3. shake well.
4. fill Rocks glass with ice strain ingredients
5. Garnish Mint Sprig
6. Enjoy the classic Whiskey Smash

Paperplane

Ingredients:
3 oz Bourbon
3/4 oz Aperol
3/4 oz Amaro Nonino
3/4 oz Fresh lemon juice

Instructions:

1. In a shaker combine ingredient
2. strain into a cocktail glass
3. Express lemon
4. enjoy!

Old Fashion

Ingredients:
2 oz Bourbon or Rye whiskey
1 sugar cube or ½ oz simple syrup
2-3 dashes Angostura bitters
-Orange twist
Large Ice Cube
Cherry for Garnish

Instructions:

1. Add Angostura bitters to the mixing glass.
2. Add Bourbon
3. Add Large Ice cube to Rocks glass.
4. Strain ingredients into rocks and stir gently.
5. Add Orange twist Garnish Cherry.
6. Enjoy the Classic Old Fashion

Whiskey Sour

Ingredients:
2 Oz bourbon or whiskey
1 oz fresh lemon juice
3/4 oz simple syrup
Garnish lemon slice and cherry
Ice

Instructions:

1. In a shaker combine bourbon, lemon juice, and simple syrup.
2. fill the shaker with ice and shake well.
3. Strain the mixture into a glass filled with ice.
4. Garnish with a lemon slice and cherry.
5. Enjoy your classic whiskey sour!

Vodka COCKTAILS

Lemon Drop

Ingredients:
1 ½ Vodka
3/4 oz Triple sec
3/4 oz fresh lemon juice
¼ oz Simple syrup

Instructions:

Simply combine all the ingredients in a shaker with ice, shake well, and strain into a chilled cocktail glass. Garnish with a lemon twist, and Sugared rim if desired.

Martini

Ingredients:
2 ½ oz Vodka
1/2 oz Dry vermouth

Instructions:

Add dry vermouth to the chilled Martini Glass dump. You should see a coated pinch of vermouth left in the glass. Add Gin to the shaker and add ice chill. Strain into Martini glass Garnish 2 olives.

Bloody Mary

Ingredients:
1 ½ oz Vodka
3 oz Tomato juice
1 dash Worcestershire sauce
1 dash Hot Sauce
Pinch of salt and pepper

Instructions:

Combine all the ingredients in a shaker with ice, shake well and strain into a glass filled with ice. Garnish with celery, olives, and lemon wedge. Oh, and tajin rim if desired.

Sex on The Beach

Ingredients:
1.5 oz Vodka
1.5 oz Peach Schnapps
2 oz Cranberry Juice
2 oz orange juice

Instructions:

Combine all ingredients in a shaker with ice, shake well and strain into a glass filled with ice. Garnish Cherry, and Orange Wedge.

Extended Vodka Cocktails

1. **Cosmopolitan:**

    - Ingredients: 1.5 oz Vodka, 0.5 oz Triple Sec, 0.5 oz Lime Juice, 1 oz Cranberry Juice.

    - Instructions: Shake all ingredients with ice, strain into a chilled cocktail glass, and garnish with a lime twist.

2. **Moscow Mule:**

    - Ingredients: 2 oz Vodka, 0.5 oz Lime Juice, Ginger Beer.

    - Instructions: Combine vodka and lime juice in a copper mug filled with ice, top with ginger beer, stir, and garnish with a lime wedge.

3. **Screwdriver:**

    - Ingredients: 1.5 oz Vodka, Orange Juice.

    - Instructions: Fill a highball glass with ice, pour vodka over ice, top with orange juice, stir gently, and garnish with an orange slice.

4. **Vodka Gimlet:**

    - Ingredients: 2 oz Vodka, 0.75 oz Lime Juice, 0.5 oz Simple Syrup.

    - Instructions: Shake all ingredients with ice, strain into a chilled cocktail glass, and garnish with a lime wheel.

5. **White Russian:**

   - Ingredients: 2 oz Vodka, 1 oz Coffee Liqueur, 1 oz Cream.

   - Instructions: Build over ice in an old-fashioned glass, stir gently, and enjoy.

6. **Espresso Martini:**

   - Ingredients: 1.5 oz Vodka, 1 oz Coffee Liqueur, 1 oz Espresso, 0.5 oz Simple Syrup.

   - Instructions: Shake all ingredients with ice, strain into a chilled cocktail glass, and garnish with coffee beans.

7. **Vodka Collins:**

   - Ingredients: 2 oz Vodka, 1 oz Lemon Juice, 0.5 oz Simple Syrup, Soda Water.

   - Instructions: Shake vodka, lemon juice, and simple syrup with ice, strain into a highball glass over ice, top with soda water, stir, and garnish with a lemon wedge.

8. **Vodka Tonic:**

   - Ingredients: 1.5 oz Vodka, Tonic Water.

   - Instructions: Fill a highball glass with ice, pour vodka over ice, top with tonic water, stir gently, and garnish with a lime wedge.

9. **French Martini:**

- Ingredients: 2 oz Vodka, 1 oz Raspberry Liqueur, 1 oz Pineapple Juice.

- Instructions: Shake all ingredients with ice, strain into a chilled cocktail glass, and garnish with a raspberry.

10. **Blue Lagoon: **

- Ingredients: 1 oz Vodka, 1 oz Blue Curacao, Lemonade.

- Instructions: Fill a glass with ice, pour vodka and blue curacao over ice, top with lemonade, stir gently, and garnish with a lemon slice.

11. **Sea Breeze: **

- Ingredients: 1.5 oz Vodka, 3 oz Cranberry Juice, 1 oz Grapefruit Juice.

- Instructions: Build over ice in a highball glass, stir gently, and garnish with a lime wedge.

12. **Black Russian: **

- Ingredients: 1.5 oz Vodka, 0.75 oz Coffee Liqueur.

- Instructions: Build over ice in an old-fashioned glass, stir gently, and enjoy.

13. **Creamsicle Cocktail: **

- Ingredients: 1.5 oz Vodka, 3 oz Orange Juice, 1 oz Cream.

- Instructions: Shake all ingredients with ice, strain into a chilled cocktail glass, and garnish with an orange slice.

14. **Vodka Cranberry: **

- Ingredients: 1.5 oz Vodka, Cranberry Juice.

- Instructions: Fill a glass with ice, pour vodka over ice, top with cranberry juice, stir gently, and garnish with a lime wedge.

15. **Bay Breeze: **

- Ingredients: 1.5 oz Vodka, 3 oz Pineapple Juice, 3 oz Cranberry Juice.

- Instructions: Build over ice in a highball glass, stir gently, and garnish with a lime wedge.

Tequila Cocktails

Margarita

Ingredients:
2 oz tequila
1 oz triple sec
1 oz fresh lime juice
salted rim

Instructions:

1. Rim a glass with salt by running a lime wedge around the edge and dipping it in salt.
2. Fill the glass with ice.
3. In a shaker, combine tequila, triple sec, and lime juice with ice. Shake well.
4. Strain the Mixture into the glass. Garnish with a lime wheel.

Paloma

Ingredients:
2 oz tequila
1/2 oz fresh lime juice
Grapefruit soda
Lime wedge for garnish

Instructions:

1. Fill a glass with ice.
2. Add Tequila and lime juice to the glass.
3. Top off with grapefruit soda and stir gently.
4. Garnish with a lime wedge.

Tequila Sunrise

Ingredients:
2 oz tequila
4 oz orange juice
½ oz grenadine
Orange slice and cherry for garnish

Instructions:

1. Fill a glass with ice.
2. Pour tequila and orange juice into the glass and stir.
3. Slowly pour grenadine over the back of a spoon to create layers.
4. garnish with an orange slice and cherry.

Mexican Mule

Ingredients:
2 oz tequila
½ oz fresh lime juice
Ginger beer
Lime wedge for garnish

Instructions:

1. Fill a copper mug with ice.
2. Add tequila and lime juice to the mug.
3. Top off with ginger beer and stir gently.
4. Garnish with a lime wedge.

Okay, so I'm going to give you guys my signature tequila cocktail drink. I'm sure you guys have heard of it before but its very popular when we make it here at Bar247 and I like to pride myself in thinking not everyone makes it like us.

Mexican Lollipop

Ingredients:
1 ½ oz Tequila
½ oz watermelon pucker (watermelon Liqueur)
fresh squeezed lime wedge
fresh squeezed lemon wedge
2 oz of sweet & Sour
Chamoy & Tajin Rim

Instructions:
1. Take a lime wedge and Rim cocktail glass
2. Add Chamoy & tajin to rim.
3. Muddle lime and lemon in cocktail glass.
4. Add 1 ½ oz tequila and ½ oz watermelon pucker.
5. add 2 oz sweet & sour.
6. Stir and enjoy the watermelon Lollipop Mexican style.

Extended Tequila Cocktails

1. ***Tequila Old Fashioned**:*
   - 2 oz Tequila

   - 1/4 oz Agave Syrup

   - 2 dashes Angostura Bitters

   - Instructions: Stir all ingredients in a glass with ice, garnish with orange twist.

2. ***Tequila Cosmopolitan**:*
   - 2 oz Tequila

   - 1 oz Cranberry Juice

   - 1/2 oz Lime Juice

   - 1/2 oz Triple Sec

   - Instructions: Shake with ice, strain into a martini glass, garnish with lime twist.

3. ***Tamarind Margarita**:*
   - 2 oz Tequila

   - 1 oz Lime Juice

   - 1 oz Tamarind Syrup

   - Instructions: Shake with ice, strain into glass, garnish with tamarind candy.

4. ***Tequila Lemonade**:*

- 2 oz Tequila

   - 4 oz Lemonade

   - 1/2 oz Simple Syrup

   - Instructions: Build in glass with ice, stir, garnish with lemon slice.

5. **Tequila Mojito**:
   - 2 oz Tequila

   - 1 oz Lime Juice

   - 6-8 Mint Leaves

   - Instructions: Muddle mint and lime, add tequila, top with soda water, stir.

6. **Piña Colada Tequila**:
   - 2 oz Tequila

   - 2 oz Pineapple Juice

   - 2 oz Coconut Cream

   - Instructions: Blend all ingredients with ice, pour into a glass, garnish with pineapple.

7. **Tequila Sangria**:
   - 2 oz Tequila

   - 4 oz Red Wine

   - 2 oz Orange Juice

- Instructions: Mix all ingredients in a pitcher with ice, stir, serve in wine glasses.

8. **Tequila Caipirinha**:
   - 2 oz Tequila

   - 1 Lime, quartered

   - 1 tbsp Sugar

   - Instructions: Muddle lime and sugar in glass, fill with ice, add tequila, stir.

9. **Spicy Tequila Pineapple Cooler**:
   - 2 oz Tequila

   - 4 oz Pineapple Juice

   - 1/2 oz Jalapeño Simple Syrup

   - Instructions: Shake with ice, strain into glass, garnish with jalapeño slice.

10. **Tequila Mint Julep**:
    - 2 oz Tequila

    - 4-6 Mint Leaves

    - 1/2 oz Simple Syrup

    - Instructions: Muddle mint and syrup, add tequila, top with crushed ice, garnish with mint.

11. **Tequila Manhattan**:
    - 2 oz Tequila

- 1 oz Sweet Vermouth

- 2 dashes Angostura Bitters

- Instructions: Stir all ingredients in a glass with ice, strain into a glass, garnish with cherry.

12. **Watermelon Tequila Cooler**:
- 2 oz Tequila

- 4 oz Watermelon Juice

- 1/2 oz Lime Juice

- Instructions: Shake with ice, strain into glass, garnish with watermelon wedge.

13. **Tequila Moscow Mule**:
- 2 oz Tequila

- 4 oz Ginger Beer

- 1/2 oz Lime Juice

- Instructions: Build in copper mug with ice, stir, garnish with lime.

14. **Tequila Blackberry Smash**:
- 2 oz Tequila

- 1 oz Blackberry Syrup

- 1/2 oz Lemon Juice

- Instructions: Shake with ice, strain into glass.

15. ***Tequila Sour***:
   - 2 oz Tequila

   - 1 oz Lemon Juice

   - 0.5 oz Simple Syrup

   - Instructions: Shake all ingredients with ice, strain into a glass filled with ice.

16. ***Tequila Old Fashioned***:
   - 2 oz Tequila, 0.25 oz Agave Syrup, Bitters, Orange Twist

   - Instructions: Stir tequila, agave syrup, and bitters with ice. Strain into glass, garnish with orange twist.

17. ***Tequila Pineapple Cocktail***:
   - 2 oz Tequila, 4 oz Pineapple Juice, 1 oz Lime Juice

   - Instructions: Shake all ingredients with ice, strain into a glass over ice.

18. ***Tequila Sunset***:
   - 2 oz Tequila, 4 oz Orange Juice, 0.5 oz Grenadine

   - Instructions: Mix tequila and orange juice, slowly pour grenadine for the sunset effect.

19. ***Tequila Cranberry Cooler***:
   - 2 oz Tequila, 4 oz Cranberry Juice, 1 oz Lime Juice

   - Instructions: Combine tequila, cranberry juice, and lime juice in a glass over ice. Stir well.

HENNESSY COCKTAILS

The Incredible Hulk

Ingredients:
- 1½ oz. Hpnotiq
- 1½ oz Hennessy
- Ice

INSTRUCTIONS

1. Fill a shaker with ice
2. add 1½ oz of Hpnotiq to the shaker.
3. pour in 1½ oz of Hennessy.
4. shake well to mix and chill the ingredients.
5. Strain the vibrant green mixture into a glass.
6. Enjoy the fruity and tropical flavors of the visually stunning Incredible Hulk Cocktail.

Hennessy Strawberry Margarita

Ingredients:
- 1½ oz of Hennessy
- ½ oz Triple Sec (orange liqueur)
- Fresh Strawberries
- Fresh Lemon
- 2 oz strawberry puree
- 2 oz Sweet & Sour Mix
- Ice

INSTRUCTIONS

1. Muddle Strawberry and Lemon in cocktail glass.
2. add 1½ oz of Hennessy
3. add ½ oz of triple sec
4. Add 2 oz of strawberry puree.
5. add 2 oz of sweet & sour mix
6. add ice.
7. Stir serve and enjoy this awesome HennyRita

Hennessy Sidecar

Ingredients:
- 2 oz Hennessy
- 3/4 oz Cointreau (orange liqueur)
- 3/4 oz fresh lemon juice
- Sugared rim
- Lemon twist for garnish
- Ice

INSTRUCTIONS

1. Rim a glass with sugar.
2. Fill a shaker with ice.
3. Add 2 oz of Hennessy to the shaker.
4. Pour in ¾ oz of Cointreau and ¾ oz of fresh lemon juice.
5. Shake well to bend the flavors.
6. Strain the mixture into the sugar-rimmed glass.
7. Garnish with a lemon twist.
8. Indulge in the elegant and citrusy notes of the Hennessy Sidecar!

Hennessy + Pineapple

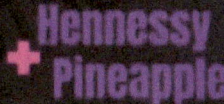 

Ingredients:
- 2 Oz of Hennessy
- 2 Oz of Pineapple Juice
- Ice

INSTRUCTIONS

1. Add 2 oz of Hennessy to cocktail glass
2. Add 2 oz of Pineapple Juice
3. Add Ice & Stir.
4. Enjoy the classic Hennessy & Pineapple.

Extended Hennessy Cocktails

1. ***Hennessy Sour***:

   - 2 oz Hennessy

   - 1 oz lemon juice

   - 0.75 oz simple syrup

   - Shake all ingredients with ice and strain into a glass. Garnish with a lemon twist.

2. ***Hennessy Old Fashioned***:

   - 2 oz Hennessy

   - 0.25 oz simple syrup

   - 2-3 dashes Angostura bitters

   - Stir ingredients with ice and strain over a large ice cube. Garnish with an orange twist.

3. ***Hennessy Mojito***:

   - 2 oz Hennessy

   - 1 oz lime juice

   - 0.5 oz simple syrup

   - Mint leaves

   - Soda water

- Muddle mint with lime juice and simple syrup, add Hennessy, top with soda water, and stir.

4. **Hennessy Ginger Ale**:

   - 2 oz Hennessy

   - Ginger ale

   - Pour Hennessy over ice in a glass, top with ginger ale, and stir gently.

5. **Hennessy Manhattan**:

   - 2 oz Hennessy

   - 1 oz sweet vermouth

   - 2-3 dashes Angostura bitters

   - Stir ingredients with ice and strain into a chilled glass. Garnish with a cherry.

6. **Hennessy Cider Punch**:

   - 2 oz Hennessy

   - Apple cider

   - Cinnamon sticks

   - Mix Hennessy and apple cider in a punch bowl, add cinnamon sticks for flavor.

7. **Hennessy Mint Julep**:

   - 2 oz Hennessy

- Mint leaves

- 0.5 oz simple syrup

- Muddle mint leaves with simple syrup, add Hennessy and crushed ice, stir gently.

8. **Hennessy Hot Toddy**:

   - 2 oz Hennessy

   - Hot water

   - Honey

   - Lemon wedge

   - Mix Hennessy with hot water, honey, and a squeeze of lemon. Garnish with a lemon wedge.

9. **Hennessy Pineapple Punch**:

   - 2 oz Hennessy

   - Pineapple juice

   - Orange juice

   - Mix Hennessy with pineapple and orange juice in a shaker with ice, strain into a glass.

10. **Hennessy Basil Smash**:

   - 2 oz Hennessy

   - Fresh basil leaves

   - 0.5 oz simple syrup

- Muddle basil with simple syrup, add Hennessy, shake with ice, and strain into a glass.

11. ***Hennessy Cosmopolitan***:

    - 2 oz Hennessy

    - 1 oz cranberry juice

    - 0.5 oz triple sec

    - 0.5 oz lime juice

    - Shake all ingredients with ice, strain into a chilled glass, and garnish with a lime twist.

12. ***Hennessy Sangria***:

    - 2 oz Hennessy

    - Red wine

    - Orange juice

    - Mixed fruits

    - Mix Hennessy, red wine, and orange juice in a pitcher with mixed fruits. Serve chilled.

13. ***Hennessy Peach Tea***:

    - 2 oz Hennessy

    - Peach schnapps

    - Iced tea

    - Lemon wedge

- Mix Hennessy, peach schnapps, and iced tea in a glass with ice. Garnish with a lemon wedge.

14. **Hennessy Irish Coffee**:

   - 2 oz Hennessy

   - Hot coffee

   - Whipped cream

   - Pour Hennessy into a cup of hot coffee, top with whipped cream.

15. **Hennessy Raspberry Fizz**:

   - 2 oz Hennessy

   - Raspberry liqueur

   - Club soda

   - Fresh raspberries

   - Mix Hennessy and raspberry liqueur in a glass with ice, top with club soda, and garnish with raspberries.

16. **Hennessy Pomegranate Punch**:

   - 2 oz Hennessy

   - Pomegranate juice

   - Sprite

   - Orange slices

   - Mix Hennessy and pomegranate juice in a punch bowl, add Sprite and orange slices for garnish.

17. **Hennessy Daiquiri**:

   - 2 oz Hennessy

   - 1 oz lime juice

   - 0.75 oz simple syrup

   - Shake all ingredients with ice and strain into a chilled glass.

18. **Hennessy Watermelon Cooler**:

   - 2 oz Hennessy

   - Watermelon juice

   - Lime juice

   - Mint leaves

   - Mix Hennessy with watermelon juice and lime juice, garnish with mint leaves.

19. **Hennessy French 75**:

   - 2 oz Hennessy

   - 1 oz lemon juice

   - 0.5 oz simple syrup

   - Champagne

   - Shake Hennessy, lemon juice, and simple syrup with ice, strain into a Champagne flute, and top with Champagne.

Rum Cocktails

—Mojito—

Ingredients:
2 oz white rum
1 oz fresh lime juice
3/4 oz simple syrup
Mint leaves
club soda
Lime wedge and mint sprig for garnish
Ice

INSTRUCTIONS

1. Muddle mint leaves and simple syrup in a glass.
2. Fill the glass with ice.
3. Pour 2 oz of white rum and 1 oz of fresh lime juice over the ice.
4. Top it off with club soda.
5. Stir gently to mix.
6. Garnish with a lime wedge and mint sprig.
7. enjoy the refreshing and minty flavors of the classic Mojito!

—Daiquiri—

Ingredients:
2 oz white rum
1 oz fresh lime juice
3/4 oz simple syrup
Lime wheel for garnish
Ice

INSTRUCTIONS

1. Fill a shaker with ice.
2. Add 2 oz of white rum.
3. Squeeze in 1 oz of fresh lime juice
4. Pour in ¾ oz of simple syrup
5. Shake well to chill the mixture.
6. strain the cocktail into a chilled glass.
7. Garnish with a lime wheel.
8. Enjoy the crisp and tangy flavors of the classic Daiquiri.

—Pina Colada—

Ingredients:
2 oz white rum
4 oz pineapple juice
2 oz coconut cream
pineapple wedge and cherry for garnish
Ice

INSTRUCTIONS

1. In a blender, combine white rum, pineapple juice, and coconut cream with ice.
2. Blend until smooth.
3. Pour the mixture into a glass.
4. Garnish with a pineapple wedge and cherry.
5. Enjoy the cream and tropical flavors of the classic Pina Colada

—Dark N Stormy—

Ingredients:
2 oz dark rum
3 oz ginger beer
Lime wedge for Garnish
ice

INSTRUCTIONS

1. Fill a glass with ice.
2. Pour 2 oz of dark rum over the ice.
3. Top it off with ginger beer.
4. Stir gently to mix.
5. Garnish with a lime wedge.
6. Enjoy the spicy and effervescent flavors of the classic Dark n Stormy!

Gin Cocktails

NEGRONI

Ingredients:
1 oz Gin
1 oz Campari
1 oz sweet vermouth
Orange twist garnish

Instructions:
1. fill the mixing glass with ice.
2. Add 1 oz of gin to the glass.
3 Pour in 1 oz of Campari.
4. Add 1 oz of sweet vermouth to the mix.
5. Stir well to combine all the ingredients.
6. Strain the mixture into a glass filled with ice.
7. garnish with an orange twist.
Enjoy the bittersweet aromatic flavors!

TOM COLLINS

Ingredients:
2 oz gin
1 oz fresh lemon juice.
1/2 oz simple syrup
club soda
Lemon wheel or wedge for garnish.
Ice

Instructions:
1. fill a shaker with ice.
2. Add 2 oz of gin to the shaker.
3. squeeze in 1 oz of fresh lemon juice.
4. Pour in ½ oz of simple syrup.
5. Shake well to combine the ingredients.
6. Strain the mixture into a Collins glass filled with ice.
7. Top it off with club soda.
8. Stir gently to mix in the club soda.
9. Garnish with a lemon wheel or wedge.
Enjoy bubbly and citrusy flavors!

GIMLET

Ingredients:
2 oz gin
1 oz fresh lime juice.
3/4 oz of simple syrup
Lime wheel or twist for garnish
ice

Instructions:
1. Fill a shaker with ice.
2. Add 2 oz of gin to the shaker.
3. squeeze in 1 oz of fresh lime juice.
4. Pour in ¾ oz of simple syrup.
5. Shake well to chill the mixture.
6. Strain the cocktail into a chilled glass.
7. Garnish with a lime wheel or twist.
Enjoy the Citrus flavors!

Extended Gin Cocktails

1. **Gin and Tonic**:
   - Ingredients:

     2 oz gin, 4 oz tonic water

   - Instructions: Pour gin over ice in a glass, top with tonic water, stir gently, garnish with a lime wedge.

2. **Martini**:
   - Ingredients:

     2.5 oz gin, 0.5 oz dry vermouth

   - Instructions: Stir gin and vermouth with ice, strain into a chilled martini glass, garnish with an olive or lemon twist.

3. **French 75**:
   - Ingredients:

     1.5 oz gin, 0.5 oz lemon juice, 0.5 oz simple syrup, champagne

   - Instructions: Shake gin, lemon juice, and simple syrup with ice, strain into a champagne flute, top with champagne, garnish with a lemon twist.

4. **Aviation**:
   - Ingredients:

     2 oz gin, 0.5 oz maraschino liqueur, 0.75 oz lemon juice

   - Instructions: Shake all ingredients with ice, strain into a glass, garnish with a cherry.

5. **Southside**:
   - Ingredients:

     2 oz gin, 0.75 oz lime juice, 0.75 oz simple syrup, mint leaves

   - Instructions: Muddle mint leaves with simple syrup, add gin, lime juice, and ice, shake, strain into a glass, garnish with a mint sprig.

6. **Corpse Reviver No. 2**:
   - Ingredients:

     1 oz gin, 1 oz Cointreau, 1 oz Lillet Blanc, 1 oz lemon juice, a dash of absinthe

   - Instructions: Shake all ingredients with ice, strain into a glass, rinse the glass with absinthe, garnish with a cherry.

7. **Ramos Gin Fizz**:
   - Ingredients:

     2 oz gin, 1 oz heavy cream, 0.5 oz lemon juice, 0.5 oz lime juice, 0.5 oz simple syrup, egg white, soda water

   - Instructions: Dry shake gin, cream, juices, syrup, and egg white, shake with ice, strain into a glass, top with soda water.

8. **Hanky Panky**:
   - Ingredients:

     1.5 oz gin, 1.5 oz sweet vermouth, 2 dashes Fernet-Branca

   - Instructions: Stir all ingredients with ice, strain into a glass, garnish with an orange twist.

9. **Bramble**:

- Ingredients:

2 oz gin, 1 oz lemon juice, 0.5 oz simple syrup, 0.5 oz blackberry liqueur

- Instructions: Shake gin, lemon juice, and syrup with ice, strain into a glass with crushed ice, drizzle blackberry liqueur, garnish with blackberries.

10. **Earl Grey Martini**:
- Ingredients:

2 oz gin, 1 oz Earl Grey tea, 0.5 oz simple syrup, lemon twist

- Instructions: Infuse gin with Earl Grey tea, stir with syrup, strain into a glass, garnish with a lemon twist.

11. **Gin Fizz**:
- Ingredients:

2 oz gin, 1 oz lemon juice, 0.5 oz simple syrup, soda water, egg white

- Instructions: Shake gin, juice, syrup, and egg white, strain into a glass, top with soda water.

12. **Sea Breeze**:
- Ingredients:

1.5 oz gin, 4 oz cranberry juice, 1 oz grapefruit juice

- Instructions: Shake gin and juices with ice, strain into a glass with ice, garnish with a lime wedge.

13. **Gin Rickey**:

- Ingredients:

    2 oz gin, 1 oz lime juice, soda water

- Instructions: Pour gin and lime juice over ice, top with soda water, stir, garnish with a lime wedge.

14. **White Lady**:
    - Ingredients:

    2 oz gin, 1 oz Cointreau, 1 oz lemon juice, egg white

- Instructions: Dry shake gin, Cointreau, lemon juice, and egg white, shake with ice, strain into a glass.

15. **Martinez**:
    - Ingredients:

    1.5 oz gin, 1.5 oz sweet vermouth, 0.25 oz maraschino liqueur, 2 dashes bitters

- Instructions: Stir all ingredients with ice, strain into a glass, garnish with a cherry.

16 **Gin Daisy**:
    - Ingredients:

    2 oz gin, 0.75 oz lemon juice, 0.5 oz grenadine, soda water

- Instructions: Shake gin, juice, and grenadine with ice, strain into a glass, top with soda water, garnish with a lemon twist.

17 **Sloe Gin Fizz**:
    - Ingredients:
        1.5 oz sloe gin, 1 oz gin, 1 oz lemon juice, 0.5 oz simple syrup, soda water

- Instructions: Shake sloe gin, gin, juice, and syrup with ice, strain into a glass, top with soda water, garnish with a lemon twist.

Beers

Okay Bartenders starting your own bar business. If you can't tell, I am extremely excited for you. I'm not going to get too much into beers, just the basics. There are so many beers out there on tap as well as bottles. Beer can be classified into various types based on factors such ingredients, brewing methods, and characteristics. Two major classifications of beer types are:

1. *Ales:*
Ales are a type of beer brewed using a warm fermentation method which results in a beer with a fruity, complex flavor profile. Ales are typically fermented at temperatures between 60-72 F (15-22 C) and are known for their diverse range of styles, including pale ales, India pale ales (IPAs), stouts, porters, and Belgian ales.

2. *Lagers:*
Lagers are a type of beer brewed using a cold fermentation process, typically at temperatures around 45-55 F (7-13 C). This method produces a beer with a clean, crisp taste and a smooth finish. The most common styles of lager include pilsners, helles, bocks, and Marzen.

These two classifications form the basis for the majority of beer styles found around the world, and they encompass a wide range of flavors, aromas, and brewing traditions.

Here are some of the glassware used when pouring beer.

Pint Glass -16 oz

Snifter - 6-22 oz
Tulip Glass - 12-16 oz
Pilsner Glass - 12-20 oz
Weizen Glass - 16-24 oz
Goblet - 10-14 oz
Mug - 12-32 oz
Flute Glass - 6-10 oz

Bring on the brewskis!

Wine

As a self-proclaimed wine connoisseur and former member of Leoness Cellars in Temecula, CA, I have had the opportunity to delve into the world of wine fermentation and production. While I may no longer have a membership at this prestigious winery, I still find myself drawn to the exquisite wines it produces. The process of wine fermentation is truly a work of art. From selecting the finest grapes to carefully monitoring the fermentation process, every step is crucial in creating the perfect bottle of wine. Whether it's a rich red or a crisp white, each type undergoes its own unique transformation before making its way to our glasses.

When entertaining guests, I always make sure to offer a variety of wines to suit every palate. From bold reds to elegant whites, there is always a wine that will appeal to every taste. The perfect bottle of wine can elevate any dining experience and create lasting memories with friends and loved ones. So, whether you're a seasoned wine enthusiast or simply looking to expand your wine knowledge, there is always a new and exciting wine waiting to be discovered. Cheers to the endless possibilities that a glass of wine can bring!

The fermentation process of red wines is a crucial step in winemaking that contributes to the rich and complex flavor characteristic of red wines. Here's an overview of the fermentation process for red wines:

1. ***Crushing and Destemming***: Red wine grapes are harvested and then crushed to release the juice and pulp. The grapes are usually destemmed to separate the stems from the grape berries.

2. ***Maceration***: The crushed grapes - including the skins, seeds, and pulp - are left to macerate in a fermentation vessel. This process allows the color, tannins, and flavors from the grape skins to leach into the juice.

3. ***Fermentation***: Yeast is added to the grape juice to initiate the fermentation process. During fermentation, yeast consumes the sugars in the juice and converts them into alcohol. This process typically takes place in stainless steel tanks or oak barrels.

4. ***Punching Down or Pumping Over***: To extract color, flavor, and tannins from the grape solids, winemakers perform either punching down (pushing down the grape cap that forms on top of the fermenting juice) or pumping over (pumping the juice over the grape cap).

5. ***Pressing***: Once fermentation is complete, the solids (skins, seeds, etc.) are separated from the liquid. The pressed juice is then transferred to another vessel for aging.

6. ***Aging:*** Red wines are often aged in oak barrels or stainless-steel tanks to develop additional complexity and flavors. This aging process can vary in length, depending on the desired style of the wine.

7. ***Bottling***: After aging, the wine is filtered, clarified, and bottled. Some red wines may continue to mature in the bottle over time, evolving in flavor and character.

   Overall, the fermentation process plays a vital role in shaping the taste, structure, and aromas of red wines. The careful management of fermentation parameters and techniques by winemakers influences the final quality and style of the wine.

The fermentation process of white wines is a key stage in winemaking that influences the flavors, aromas, and characteristics of the final wine. Here's an overview of the fermentation process for white wines:

1. *Harvesting and Crushing*: White wine grapes are harvested and quickly transported to the winery to preserve their freshness. The grapes are then gently crushed to release the juice while minimizing skin contact, which helps maintain the wine's light color.

2. *Pressing*: Once the grapes are crushed, the juice is separated from the skins, seeds, and solids through pressing. This process ensures that only the juice, which is high in sugars and flavors, is used for fermentation.

3. *Settling and Clarification*: The juice may undergo settling to allow solids to settle at the bottom of the container. This helps clarify the juice before fermentation begins, contributing to the wine's clarity and stability.

4. *Cooling and Inoculation*: The clarified juice is often cooled to a specific temperature to prevent oxidation and preserve the delicate aromas. Yeast strains, either native or selected, are then added to initiate fermentation.

5. *Fermentation*: The yeast consumes the sugars in the juice and converts them into alcohol. Fermentation for white wines typically occurs at lower temperatures compared to red wines to retain freshness and fruitiness.

6. *Aging and Sur Lie*: After fermentation, some white wines undergo aging on the lees (dead yeast cells) to enhance texture and complexity. This process, known as "sur lie," involves stirring the lees into the wine to extract additional flavors and mouthfeel.

7. *Malolactic Fermentation* (Optional): Some white wines, particularly full-bodied styles like Chardonnay, may undergo malolactic fermentation, where tart malic acid is converted into softer lactic acid. This process can impart a creamy texture and buttery notes to the wine.

8. *Filtration and Stabilization*: Before bottling, white wines are often filtered to remove any remaining solids and ensure clarity. Stabilization processes may also be employed to prevent unwanted chemical reactions or microbial growth in the bottle.

9. *Bottling*: Once the winemaker is satisfied with the wine's flavor profile and stability, the wine is bottled and corked. White wines are ready to be enjoyed upon release or may benefit from additional bottle aging for certain styles.

The fermentation process for white wines is a delicate dance of preserving the grapes' natural flavors and aromas while allowing the yeast to work its magic in creating a balanced and refreshing final product. Each step, from grape selection to bottling, influences the overall character of the white wine and showcases the winemaker's skill and vision.

Here are four well-known white wine varieties that are popular among wine enthusiasts:

1. *Chardonnay*: Chardonnay is one of the most widely planted white wine grape varieties globally. It produces a diverse range

of styles, from crisp and unoaked wines with notes of green apple and citrus to rich and buttery expressions aged in oak barrels.

2. **Sauvignon Blanc**: Sauvignon Blanc is known for its vibrant acidity and distinctive aromas of grapefruit, tropical fruits, and fresh-cut grass. This white wine is often enjoyed young to savor its zesty and refreshing characteristics.

3. **Riesling**: Riesling is a versatile white wine grape that can produce a wide spectrum of styles, from bone-dry to lusciously sweet. It is prized for its floral aromas, high acidity, and flavors that range from citrus and stone fruits to honey and petrol notes.

4. **Pinot Grigio/Pinot Gris**: Pinot Grigio (Italian) or Pinot Gris (French) is a popular white wine known for its light, crisp, and easy-drinking qualities. It typically displays flavors of citrus, pear, and apple, making it a refreshing choice for various occasions.

These white wine varieties offer a diverse range of flavors, styles, and characteristics, appealing to a broad spectrum of wine preferences. Whether you enjoy a bright and citrusy Sauvignon Blanc or a complex and oaky Chardonnay, there is a white wine option to suit every palate.

Here are four well-known red wine varieties that are popular among wine enthusiasts:

1. **Cabernet Sauvignon**: Cabernet Sauvignon is one of the most widely recognized red wine grape varieties. It is known for producing full-bodied wines with rich flavors of dark fruits, cassis, and hints of oak. Cabernet Sauvignon wines often exhibit firm tannins and aging potential.

2. ***Merlot***: Merlot is a versatile red wine grape that produces smooth and approachable wines with flavors of ripe plums, red berries, and a velvety texture. Merlot wines are often characterized by their soft tannins and balanced fruit-forward profile.

3. ***Pinot Noir***: Pinot Noir is renowned for its elegance, complexity, and transparency of terroir. It often showcases delicate flavors of red fruits, earthy notes, and a silky texture. Pinot Noir wines can range from light and fruity to more robust and structured.

4. ***Syrah/Shiraz***: Syrah (known as Shiraz in Australia) is a bold and spicy red wine grape that produces wines with intense flavors of black pepper, dark fruits, and smoky notes. Syrah/Shiraz wines can vary in style from elegant and peppery to robust and full-bodied.

These red wine varieties offer a diverse array of flavors, textures, and styles, appealing to a wide range of wine preferences. Whether you prefer the structured tannins of Cabernet Sauvignon, the softness of Merlot, the finesse of Pinot Noir, or the boldness of Syrah/Shiraz, there is a red wine option to suit every palate.

When it comes to pairing wines with dinner, versatility and balance are key. Here are four well-known dinner wines that complement a variety of dishes across different cuisines:

1. ***Chardonnay***: Chardonnay is a popular dinner wine choice due to its versatility and ability to pair well with a wide range of dishes. Whether you're having roasted chicken, seafood, pasta with creamy sauces, or a light salad, a well-balanced

Chardonnay with notes of citrus, oak, and butter can be a delightful companion.

2. ***Pinot Noir***: Pinot Noir is an excellent dinner wine option known for its food-friendly character. This red wine's delicate flavors of red fruits, earthy notes, and silky texture make it a great match for dishes like roasted duck, salmon, mushroom risotto, or even a simple cheese platter.

3. ***Sauvignon Blanc***: Sauvignon Blanc is a refreshing white wine that pairs well with a variety of dinner dishes, especially those with vibrant flavors and fresh ingredients. Whether you're enjoying a light salad, grilled fish, vegetable stir-fry, or seafood pasta, the zesty acidity and tropical fruit notes of Sauvignon Blanc can enhance the meal.

4. ***Cabernet Sauvignon***: Cabernet Sauvignon is a classic dinner wine choice that complements hearty dishes with robust flavors. Whether you're serving grilled steak, lamb chops, beef stew, or a rich mushroom lasagna, the bold dark fruit flavors, firm tannins, and hints of oak in Cabernet Sauvignon can stand up to the richness of the meal.

These four dinner wines offer a range of flavors, textures, and profiles that can elevate the dining experience and enhance the flavors of various dishes. Whether you're having a casual weeknight dinner or a special occasion meal, these wines can bring balance and enjoyment to the table.

If you haven't been wine tasting, you gots to try it! Even if it's just for the vibe.

MISSION + VISION

"At BAR 247, our mission is to create a fun and satisfying experience for our customers by transforming their parties and events into magical settings. With our classic cocktails, themed events, and custom menus tailored to each experience, we aim to bring joy and delight to every gathering.

Through our warm smiles and exceptional customer service, we strive to exceed expectations, leaving our customers wowed and eager to refer us to their family and friends."

Laws & Regulations

When serving alcohol in the state of California, it is important to follow a set of laws and regulations that govern the sale and consumption of alcohol. These laws are in place to ensure the safety and well-being of the public, as well as to prevent underage drinking and overconsumption.

Some general guidelines to keep in mind when serving alcohol in California include:

- The legal drinking age in California is 21, and it is illegal to serve alcohol to anyone under this age.
- It is illegal to serve alcohol to someone who is visibly intoxicated or to allow individuals to become intoxicated on your premises.
- Servers and bartenders must be properly trained in responsible alcohol service and must be able to recognize the signs of intoxication.
- It is illegal to serve alcohol without a valid license or permit.
- Alcohol must be served in a responsible manner, with measures in place to prevent overconsumption, such as offering food or non-alcoholic beverages.
- There are strict regulations regarding the hours of alcohol service, with most establishments required to stop serving alcohol by 2 a.m.

By following these laws and regulations, you can help ensure a safe and enjoyable experience for your customers while staying in compliance with the state's alcohol serving laws.

Be sure to check your States Laws and Regulations.

RBS Training

Okay guys, on to some fun stuff, RBS certification - which stands for Responsible Beverage Service. Most states are now requiring it to serve alcohol. I am in the state of California, and we require it. As of now it's about $40 bucks. It's a training class you can take online, but very lengthy, so have sometime set aside. This will be good for you as individual bartenders and also if you have your own business when getting booked at event spaces. They definitely want to see this. I have dropped the link below for the state of California. Outside of Cali you can search your governments alcoholic beverage website to find out where you can take the training and exam, along with the steps to guide to the right place

Don't be overwhelmed by this. All of this is worth the big bucks you're about to start making. Nobody really knows how much bartenders make until they know somebody who knows somebody; but trust and believe, it's lit! Lol!

Obtaining an RBS (Responsible Beverage Service) certification is a relatively straightforward process that involves completing a training program designed to educate individuals on responsible alcohol service practices. Here are the general steps to obtain an RBs certification:

1. **Research Requirements**: Start by researching the specific RBS certification requirements in your state or jurisdiction. Each location may have varying regulations and approved training providers for RBS certification.

2. **Select an Approved Training Provider**: Choose an approved training provider that offers an RBS certification

course. These courses are typically available through in-person classes, online platforms, or a combination of both.

3. **Enroll in the Course**: Enroll in the RBS certification course offered by the approved training provider. Ensure that the course meets the requirements set forth by your state or jurisdiction for certification.

4. **Complete the Training**: Participate in and complete the RBS certification training program. The course will cover topics such as alcohol laws and regulations, recognizing signs of intoxication, handling difficult situations, and preventing underage drinking.

5. **Pass the Exam (if required) **: Some RBS certification programs may include a final exam to test your knowledge of responsible alcohol service practices. Make sure to study and prepare for the exam to successfully pass and earn your certification.

6. **Receive Your Certification**: Upon successfully completing the training and any required exam, you will receive your RBS certification. This certification may come in the form of a physical certificate or a digital badge, depending on the training provider.

7. **Renew and Stay Updated**: RBS certifications typically have an expiration date, so it's important to keep track of when your certification needs to be renewed. Stay informed about any changes in alcohol service regulations to ensure ongoing compliance.

By following these steps and completing an approved RBS certification training program, you can obtain the necessary certification to serve alcohol responsibly and legally. This certification not only enhances your skills as a bartender but also demonstrates your commitment to upholding high standards of alcohol service in the industry.

https://abcbiz.abc.ca.gov/

Signs of Intoxication

You all will go through some of this in your RBS training and will definitely experience it for yourselves (lol), but I'm going to give it to you straight. The first sign is the person coming up to the bar already complaining about how you make it before you can pour it. Then when they see you poured a decent or right amount, they'll come back and be like - in a loud obnoxious voice - make my drink that same way. Or if they didn't like the way you poured it, they'll be like - I can't taste nothing, can you pour some more? Those are the ones who will be the first ones to fall on their face or you'll see them on the dance floor acting a fool. I can't make this up.

Depending on where you work you may not always cut ppl off after 2 drinks, but make sure y'all follow those laws and regulations and use your best judgement - because you and both the business could be sued. Always offer guest water, food if possible, and an Uber. Please don't be afraid to cut nobody off. Trust me, most people will thank you in the end; and the ones who don't, oh well. I saved your life is the attitude to keep.

Another sign is someone being irate right off the back. You want to cut them off right away because they are acting off emotions, which can be very dangerous because alcohol can sometimes make things worse. As you work and get used to the industry, you'll see your own signs of intoxication and know it's cut off time. Y'all remember that song by Tupac? It's Check out time! We gotta go! Lol!

Drink Responsibly

    This is the season. Unpopular Opinion. My friends always laugh at me with my different seasons for drinking certain spirits. I am mostly a tequila girl. However, I love whiskey during winter. I like to tell my guests to stay away from the Henn doggy dog during summer. It's too hot, and that's how fights break out. Lol… kidding not kidding! You must be smart out here though. So, Vodka and Gin in spring. Tequila, spring/summer. Rum is cool for the summer as long as you're super hydrated. Anything dark, such as Whiskey and Cognac, save that for winter. And Please Drink Responsibly. If you are having a bad day, stay away from the booze hydrate and recalibrate.

Love always!
Jessica Jones
Bar247

Difficult Customers

    Really briefly - not too much energy on this - I would like to address there will be difficult customers sometimes. That's their personality; and sometimes they're having a bad day and come to the bar for a drink, duh! Lol! But you have to have tough skin to be a bartender. You're constantly going to get hit on, male or female. Some people are going to be rude because again, they don't know how much money we make and that we are some bosses. But stay in character.

    One of my server friends David from LAX told me one time all servers and bartenders are fake. Sometimes we have to be. Also, you must have a sense of integrity you know. Always do the right thing, even when no one is looking. So ignore that rude customer, because you never know what someone is going through. We all done had a bad day. If they become irate, call security or somebody to deescalate and even remove the customer. You got this!

My Life Before Bartending. Let Me Tell You!

Before I found my passion for bartending, my journey was filled with uncertainty and a constant search for my true calling. After graduating high school, I attended a trade school with dreams of becoming a flight attendant, only to realize it wasn't the right fit for me. Feeling lost and homesick, I left the job after two years. I then tried my hand at different jobs, from making appointments at State Farm to working at Kaiser through temp agencies. Despite the variety of roles I took on, I always felt a desire to be my own boss and serve others in a more meaningful way.

In 2013, everything changed when I decided to enroll in bartending school. Riverside National Bartending School provided me with the skills and confidence I needed to pursue a career in bartending. After completing the program, I landed my first bartending job at LAX airport, where I gained valuable experience in the industry.

Despite the challenges I faced, I never lost sight of my dream to start my own business. In 2018, I took a leap of faith and launched my mobile bar service. With the support of my community and the love of my customers, my business has thrived beyond my wildest dreams.

I share my story to inspire others to never give up on themselves, no matter how many obstacles they may face. It's essential to silence the doubts and fears that hold us back and pursue our passions wholeheartedly. The journey may be challenging, but the rewards of following your dreams are worth it in the end.

Quotes From My Favorite Authors

I aim to provide my readers with some inspiring quotes from my favorite authors. These quotes have personally helped me to stay focused, push through distractions, and remember that it's never too late to start over. I hope these words of wisdom will provide you with the same motivation and encouragement.

"Success is doing what you want to do, when you want, where you want, with whom you want, as much as you want." - Tony Robbins

"Don't take anything personally. Nothing others do is because of you. What others say and do is a projection of their own reality." - Don Miguel Ruiz

"The willingness to do hard things opens great windows of opportunity" - Mel Robbins

"Formal Education will make you a living; self-education will make you a fortune" - Jim Rohn

"If you want to stand out, don't blend in. You were born to stand out." - Jim Kwik

"I am so happy and grateful now-that money comes to me in increasing quantities through multiple sources on a continuous basis. – Bob Proctor

"Do not be anxious about anything but in everything, by prayer and supplication with Thanksgiving let your request be made

known to God, and the peace of God which surpasses all understanding will guard your hearts and minds in Christ Jesus.
- Apostle Paul; Philippians 4:6-7

TEAM WORK
MAKES THE DREAM WORK

With a strong team by your side, success is almost guaranteed. I would like to express my gratitude to the individuals who have been with me from the beginning at Bar247 - Kharah Black, Linnea Charles, Mya Musgrove, Mia Black, and all the new team members. Your dedication and support have been invaluable to me, and I couldn't have done it without you. Thank you for standing by me every step of the way and for imparting your knowledge and skills to help us stay ahead of the game.

Building a team requires self-awareness and honesty as a leader. It is essential to always present yourself authentically and to ensure that every member of your team looks and feels like a boss. Empowering your team members to excel and contribute to the success of the business is crucial. Remember, there is an abundance of opportunities in this industry for everyone to thrive.

Before hiring new team members, consider carefully what qualities you are looking for in an employee. Each position in your team should be filled by an individual who excels in that specific role. Whether it's an outgoing bartender, a by-the-book bartender, a fashionista bartender, or an event designer, each member should bring their unique strengths and skills to the table.

I have complete confidence in my team, which allows me to step back and focus on the bigger picture. Their dedication and professionalism make it possible for me to trust that everything will run smoothly even in my absence. I am truly grateful for each and every member of our team.

As we continue to grow and expand, I am excited to see what the future holds for us. I have a team of talented and dedicated individuals who are capable of achieving great things both collectively and individually. Together, we are unstoppable.

Follow us on Instagram: @_bar247 | Our website: bar247.co | Linktree: linktr.ee/Bar247

Wrap Up

As I wrap up this book on becoming your own boss, specifically a mobile bartending boss, I would like to discuss distractions. They will always be here to trip you up. But you've got to keep pushing, that's the only way you win. Never give up on you. Remember life and death is in the power of the tongue, and those who love it eat its fruit. I hope you eat the fruit of a good life, healthy, wealthy, perseverance, love, joy, and endurance. Focus only on the things you can control like your emotions and decision making. Make the decision to continue with integrity, and good character.

Now go get that bag! It's Lit!
My voice.

www.ingramcontent.com/pod-product-compliance
Lightning Source LLC
Chambersburg PA
CBHW071840210526
45479CB00001B/225